THE BATTLE OF ACTIUM

The End of the Roman Civil Wars

Written by Cédric Bernardi
In collaboration with Nicolas Cartelet
Translated by Carly Probert

History **50MINUTES**.com

THE BATTLE OF ACTIUM

KEY INFORMATION

- **When:** 2 September, 31 B.C.
- **Where:** Near Actium, Greece
- **Context:** The civil war between Octavius and Mark Antony
- **Belligerents:** Octavius and his supporters against Mark Anthony, Egypt and their supporters
- **Commanders and leaders:**
  - Octavius, Roman politician (63 B.C.-14 A.D.)
  - Marcus Vipsanius Agrippa, Roman general and politician (63-12 B.C.)
  - Mark Antony, Roman politician (83-30 B.C.)
  - Cleopatra, Queen of Egypt (c. 69-30 B.C.)
- **Outcome:** Victory for Octavius
- **Victims:**
  - Octavius' camp: it is impossible to estimate losses
  - Mark Antony and Cleopatra's camp: approximately 5 000 deaths

INTRODUCTION

On 2 September 31 B.C., the fate of the Roman Republic was settled at Actium, off the Greek coast. Two Roman generals clashed at sea, fighting for the supreme power, with Octavius on the one side, son of Julius Caesar and defender of Rome, and Mark Antony on the other, who made Alexandria his capital. The civil war legacy of the conflict between Julius Caesar (Roman statesman, 100/101-44 B.C.)

and Pompey (Roman statesman, 106-48 B.C.) reached its culmination.

13 years after the assassination of Julius Caesar, the Battle of Actium brought an end to a long period of internal conflicts within the Republic. The old aristocratic regime, which allowed the Senate to temper the enthusiasm of the ambitious, gradually crumbled during the 1st century B.C., leaving great generals with the means to control Rome. The victory of Octavius, who later took the name of Augustus and became the first Roman emperor, was the culmination of the process of the centralization of power and the lowering of senatorial prerogatives.

But, beyond the fight between two men, Actium also symbolized the clash between two worlds. Taking over from Julius Caesar, Octavius was a defender of the Roman power. Mark Antony, triumvir of rich but eastern territories, joined forces with the Egyptian Cleopatra and appeared as a Hellenistic monarch, breaking away from Rome's authority. Faced with the fight between these two men, the ancient commentators believed they were attending the fratricidal struggle between the East and the West. The story is well known: the West emerged victorious, ensuring Roman domination in the Mediterranean for hundreds of years.

POLITICAL AND SOCIAL CONTEXT

AN ASSASSINATION WITH HEAVY CONSEQUENCES

In 31 B.C., Rome had fallen prey to civil war for decades. Well before the Battle of Actium, several major politicians had competed to obtain supreme power. In the mid-1st century B.C., Julius Caesar managed to defeat his rivals: Pompey, Cato of Utica (95-46 B.C.) and even Metellus Scipio (who died in 46 B.C.) were all defeated. Although he had become the absolute master of Rome, Julius Caesar, at the Roman Senate, was stabbed to death on 15 March 44 B.C. This assassination plot was led by Gaius Cassius Longinus (who died in 42 B.C.) and Marcus Junius Brutus (85-42 B.C.), Caesar's adopted heir.

The Death of Caesar, painting by Jean-Léon Gérôme, 1867.

At that time, Mark Antony was still the faithful lieutenant of the late statesman, while Octavius was his nephew. Neither of them took part in the plot and they mourned the death of the dictator as his true friends. At the funeral, Antony spoke directly to the Roman people and managed to move them into remembering the military glory of the deceased. He also took the opportunity to openly accuse Marcus Junius Brutus and Gaius Cassius Longinus. Moved by the speech, the crowd reacted violently: revolts broke out all over the city and the houses of the two culprits were burned down.

GOOD TO KNOW

The assassination of Julius Caesar was fomented by a group of aristocrats in response to the great power that the dictator had obtained from the Senate. The conspirators hoped to liberate Rome from a tyrant and obtain the full support of the people in exchange for this service to the homeland. Marcus Junius Brutus, carrying out the fatal blow to his adoptive father, betrayed his own, but remained faithful to the Republic. Seeing his son among the killers, Julius Caesar is reported to have said, according to Suetonius (Latin historian, 69-126): "You too, my son."

Unfortunately for him, Mark Antony was quicker to influence public opinion and denounce an infamous plot: the two murderers were forced to leave Rome and take refuge in the East.

At the time, Antony was in Rome while Octavius was in Greece. When he learned of the sad news, he quickly returned: before dying, Julius Caesar had made him the heir of all his property. He thus became the most powerful man in Rome, as he obtained all the riches and the clientele of the deceased. As for Mark Antony, he remained the most popular. The rivalry between the two men was only just beginning.

AN ALLIANCE OF TRIUMVIRATES AGAINST MARCUS JUNIUS BRUTUS AND GAIUS CASSIUS LONGINUS

In 43 B.C., three men decided to join forces in order to defeat Marcus Junius Brutus and Gaius Cassius Longinus, who had reformed an army in Asia. The second triumvirate was born.

GOOD TO KNOW

A triumvirate was a political and military alliance created between three people. In 43 B.C., Mark Antony, Octavius and Lepidus (died c. 13 B.C.), a close friend of Julius Caesar, concluded this alliance. The triumvirs gained important powers for five renewable years: in particular, they were allowed to make a list of opponents whose property would be forfeited to Rome. This alliance was essential for defeating the murderers of Julius Caesar and preventing them from returning to Italy. Mark Antony and Octavius were forced to ally themselves, as they knew they could not defeat them

Mark Antony and Octavius then went to fight in Greece after concluding their alliance. The meeting took place in Philippi (Macedonia) in 42 B.C.: Mark Antony managed to defeat Marcus Junius Brutus and Gaius Cassius Longinus, who chose to commit suicide rather than surrender, while Octavius was ill during the battle. The honor of victory was therefore almost exclusively Mark Antony's.

Subsequently, the three men renewed their alliance and shared the Roman world between them:

- Africa was given to Lepidus;
- The Western provinces (Italy, Gaul and Spain) were given to Octavius;
- The richer provinces (Greece, Egypt and Minor Asia) were awarded to Mark Antony.

At first, they administered political affairs on equal footing. Yet, each of them was already looking to satisfy their personal ambitions and hold the means to prevail over their rivals. Their apparent unity was reinforced by marriage in 40 B.C., when Mark Antony married Octavia (70-11 B.C.), the sister of Octavius.

Four years later, Octavius accused Lepidus of overstepping his mark and dismissed him from office. Now there were only two triumvirs to compete for supremacy. But, instead of sharing Africa and the army of Lepidus with Mark Antony in accordance with the principle of equality between the three men, Octavius took them for his own. Mark Antony complained of this abuse, without success: tensions began to arise between them.

MARK ANTONY IN THE EAST

Ancient sources view the departure of Mark Antony to the East as the cause of his sad destiny. Indeed, this region was considered by the Romans to be a land of debauchery and lust, which weakened the body and the mind. For instance, it is reported that Mark Antony gave in to the sweetness of Greek life. These testimonies are partially incorrect, as the Roman general also took the time to prepare a major campaign against the Parthians.

GOOD TO KNOW

The Parthians were a very powerful people living in ancient Persia (modern-day Iran, Iraq and Afghanistan). At the time of Mark Antony, they were formidable opponents for Rome. Indeed, in 53 B.C., they killed about 20 000 Roman soldiers during the Battle of Carrhae, by routing the forces of Marcus Licinius Cassius (115-53 B.C.). As soon as he took office in the East, Mark Antony planned to avenge this insult.

Busy making preparations, Mark Antony summoned Cleopatra to Cilicia (area south of modern day Turkey) so that she could explain her reasons for providing aid to

Marcus Junius Brutus and Gaius Cassius Longinus after the assassination of Julius Caesar. Aware of the diplomatic stakes of this meeting, the queen of Egypt undertook to seduce Mark Antony, as she had done before with Julius Caesar. Their meeting took place on the young woman's ship, where he was given a sumptuous feast. The meeting was successful and the triumvir quickly fell in love with this queen, who was said to be refined and full of wit. For many ancient historians, this union marked the enslavement of Mark Antony to oriental delights even more: Cleopatra would have stifled the nobility and the virtue of the Roman.

The Meal of Marc Antony and Cleopatra, painting by Charles-Joseph Natoire, 1754.

Despite his love for Cleopatra and the pleasures of an

idle life, Mark Antony remained determined to launch his legions in the assault on the Parthian Empire. In retrospect, his campaign appeared as a disastrous enterprise. In 37 B.C., he left with his army composed of about 70 000 men, but was stopped by the severe winter of the Armenian mountains and his failure at the siege of Phraaspa (36 B.C.). He had to turn back and narrowly escaped death. The results of this disastrous campaign were heavy: 25 000 Roman casualties were added to the 8 000 who died from the cold. In Rome, Octavius and his allies were convinced that this defeat was due to the passion that Mark Antony felt towards Cleopatra. They also claimed that the general, in his eagerness to find his mistress, was responsible for the loss of the 8 000 men, having pushed his troops beyond reason. Therefore, Octavius could not forgive this shameful campaign. However, Mark Antony tried to obliterate his defeat by making another attempt to attack the Parthian territory the following year, but he failed again and made up for it by invading Armenia, which at the time was Rome's ally. Following this minor victory, he held a triumph in Alexandria: for the first time in history, a Roman general chose to organize a triumph outside of Italy. From then on, Mark Antony lived in Alexandria, the capital of the kingdom of Egypt, and he became more and more like a Hellenistic monarch.

THE ROMAN AND THE EGYPTIAN

Little by little, Mark Antony made unbearable decisions for the Romans. Indeed, after his triumph, he offered Roman territories to the three children he had with Cleopatra.

Armenia, Phoenicia, Syria and Cilicia were given in succession: thus, it was the Egyptian queen who became the de facto owner of these lands. In Rome, these measures were considered to be insults. Added to this was the insult this caused to Octavius' family, since he was still married to Octavia.

One must not underestimate the rivalry that existed between the two women: this forms part of the causes of the future conflict between Mark Antony and Octavius. Indeed, Octavia behaved like a perfect wife, and the many humiliations she suffered from her husband raised tensions with Octavius. The situation did not improve in 32 B.C. when Mark Antony repudiated her. This was too much for Octavius who took his *casus belli*: the battle was now inevitable.

THE ORIGINS OF THE WAR: THE WILL OF MARK ANTONY

For the war to begin, Octavius still needed to convince the Senate to take part in his campaign. It was for this purpose that he disclosed the contents of Mark Antony's will, in which his donations to the children he had with Cleopatra were specified. The general had also named his successor as none other than Caesarion, son of Julius Caesar, and stated that he wished to be buried in Alexandria and not in Rome, as tradition dictated. From then on, Mark Antony was seen by all as an Oriental prince and an enemy of Rome.

In this political conflict, Octavius presented himself as a victim, offended by the repudiation of his sister. Moreover, he presented himself as a guarantor of Roman traditions and claimed to defend the interests of Rome against the East. The reading of Mark Antony's will caused the desired effect: in Rome, those who were still undecided ranked themselves definitively on the side of Octavius. It should be noted that in 32 B.C., the war was not declared against Mark Antony, but against Cleopatra, the true cause of the war in the eyes of the Romans. However, although Octavius pretended to be the enemy of this queen who was eager for conquests, he also used this conflict as an opportunity to get rid of the last opponent to his hegemony.

COMMANDERS AND LEADERS

OCTAVIUS, ROMAN POLITICIAN

Octavius (Gaius Octavius Thurinus), also known as Octavian, was born in 63 B.C. He was 32 years old when the Battle of Actium broke out. He was the great-nephew of Julius Caesar and his adopted heir after his death. Initially allied with Mark Antony, they formed a triumvirate with Lepidus in order to defeat the killers of Julius Ceasar. After Marcus Junius Brutus and Gaius Cassius Longinus were defeated, Mark Antony and Octavius were alone in the race for supreme power. In the 30s B.C., a constant rivalry developed between the two men and a war soon became inevitable. Publicly humiliated by Mark Antony after the repudiation of his sister, Octavius declared war on the Egyptian queen Cleopatra, following the reading of Mark Antony's will to the Senate of Rome.

At Actium, on 2 September 31 B.C., the two men clashed in a decisive battle, in which Octavius was the clear winner. After landing in Egypt the following year, he saw that Mark Antony and Cleopatra had committed suicide in turn, thus leaving him to become the sole owner of absolute power in Rome. On 16 January 27 B.C., Octavius took the nickname of Augustus and introduced a new form of government: the principate. Now without rival and proud to have brought an end to the civil wars, he could become the Roman emperor in peace. He remained on the imperial throne for more than 41 years.

Augustus died in the year 14 A.D. at the age of 77, leaving behind a Roman empire that was more powerful and prosperous than ever before.

MARCUS VIPSANIUS AGRIPPA, ROMAN GENERAL AND POLITICIAN

Marcus Vipsanius Agrippa, a member of the small Roman aristocracy, was born in 63 B.C. A soldier by trade, he was a close friend of Octavius in his youth. In 44 B.C., when Julius Caesar was assassinated, he was already at the future emperor's side. Gradually, he acted as the armed wing of Octavius, in the name of whom he won two important victories over political rivals: Pompey and Mark Antony.

As an advisor, he accessed the upper echelons of Roman power. He participated in the establishment of the principate and was appointed consul in 37 and 28 B.C. He became even closer to the emperor by marrying his daughter Julia (39 B.C.-14 A.D.). He fought for Rome until the end of his life and conquered Hispania and the barbarian territories located on the Danube. He died in 12 B.C. and received the glory of a burial in the emperor's mausoleum.

MARK ANTONY, ROMAN POLITICIAN

Mark Antony (Marcus Antonius), the son of Antonius Creticus (Praetor, who died in 75 B.C.), was born in 86 or 83 B.C. In 40 B.C., he sided with Julius Caesar in his struggle against Pompey. Having defeated the assassins of the dictator, Antony allied with Octavius and received the Roman provinces of the East such as Syria, Judea and Minor Asia. In Egypt, he led several disastrous campaigns against the Parthians and met Cleopatra, with whom he fell in love. They had a passionate relationship in Alexandria, despite his marriage to the sister of Octavius.

DID YOU KNOW?

To win the loyalties of the Eastern countries, Mark Antony developed a Hellenistic strategy from Egypt. He lived in Alexandria and gave his children Greek and Oriental names: Alexander (in honor of Alexander the Great, 356-323 B.C.), Ptolemy (the traditional name of Egyptian kings) and Cleopatra. Moreover, he distributed Roman possessions to regional princes in order to make them clients. Finally, he sought to follow in the footsteps of Alexander the Great by leading his armies to the east. This "Eastern" attitude would end his popularity in Rome.

A few years later, having repudiated Octavia and illegally distributed Roman possessions to the children he had with Cleopatra, Mark Antony knew that a war was inevitable. When the Battle of Actium took place, he was over 50 years old, 20 years older than his young rival. Defeated and humiliated by his cowardly behavior – he fled from the fighting –, Mark Antony ended up committing suicide in 30 B.C. in Alexandria, as he was about to be taken prisoner by Octavius.

CLEOPATRA, QUEEN OF EGYPT

Cleopatra, the daughter of the Egyptian king Ptolemy XII Auletes (95-51 B.C.) was born in 69 B.C. Few Egyptian sources mention her life. All that is known of her originates from the victor of Actium. Yet, she appears as one of the most important female figures in the history of the Antiquity. The mistress of Julius Caesar, with who she had a son named Caesarion, she became the queen of a powerful vassal kingdom of Rome, Egypt.

The relationship between Cleopatra and Mark Antony became legendary, as it was one of the main causes of the war between Egypt and Rome and the peak of the rivalry between Mark Antony and Octavius. The queen was present in the Battle of Actium and her sudden flight played a decisive role in the outcome of the conflict. Defeated by the Roman army, she finally committed suicide in 30 B.C., shortly after Mark Antony. Her death also remains engraved in collective memory: while taking her last meal with her two faithful servants, she was brought a basket of figs, inside which an asp (term used in Egypt to refer to the Egyptian cobra) was hidden. After being bitten by this snake in the breast or arm, Cleopatra died, choosing a noble death over a shameful parade behind the chariot of Octavius in his future triumph. More than a historical figure, Cleopatra has become a prominent figure over the centuries, who still fascinates even 21 centuries after her death.

ANALYSIS OF THE BATTLE

MARK ANTONY'S PREPARATIONS

In 32 B.C., when Mark Antony learned of the war declaration on Cleopatra from Rome, he went to Ephesys (Minor Asia city) with the Queen of Egypt, in preparation for the confrontation. Although the war had not been declared on him personally and he could therefore still change sides, he chose not to abandon his lover. Therefore, preparations were well underway in both camps: troops and mercenaries were enlisted and taxes were raised in the Roman cities.

Soon, the battle appeared to be a confrontation between the East and the West. The whole of Italy, but also Gaul, Spain and Libya, openly supported Octavius. As for Mark Antony, he was supported by the Eastern nations: Syria, Judea, Arabia and Minor Asia joined his camp. Recognizing this as a decisive battle, Cleopatra asked all kings and princes of the East under Roman or Egyptian rule to provide Mark Antony with what he needed to carry out this war.

GOOD TO KNOW

Although Octavius presented himself as the sole defender of Roman interests against the greed of Cleopatra and Egypt, Mark Antony, meanwhile, publicly swore to his soldiers – who were mostly Roman – that this was not a war against their homeland. He promised them that, in the case of victory, he would discharge his command and hand over the power to the hands of the Senate and the people of Rome. He therefore sought to present himself as a staunch defender of the Republic, not a traitor to his country. Moreover, he accused Octavius of manipulating the people to satisfy his inordinate ambition. Mark Antony insisted on this fundamental difference that Octavius was fighting to become the supreme master, while he was fighting for the freedom of all, beginning with the Roman people.

In 32 B.C., Mark Antony received many goods from Cleopatra: 200 ships were added to the 300 they already possessed. She also gave him money and food for his army and decided to go with him to Greece. After gathering their forces, the two lovers directed the large fleet to Athens, where they stopped for several weeks. Latin historians claim that Mark Antony then lost himself in lavish parties, to the astonishment of his soldiers because no victory had been won so far.

OCTAVIUS' PREPARATIONS

Initially, Octavius was surprised by the speed with which Mark Antony was preparing for war. When his rival left Egypt, he had yet to control a revolt in Italy, born from the tax he raised to finance the war. Fearing that the fighting would take place on Italian soil, Octavius first appeared to be overwhelmed by the events. Fortunately for him, Mark Antony stopped for a long time in Athens, thus delaying his attack.

It was in 31 B.C. that Mark Antony resumed his march towards the west and had his fleet berthed at Actium, at the entrance of the Ambracian Gulf (northwest of Acarnania, Greece). This place was not chosen at random: it offered a harbor enabling the anchoring of vessels before the assault. Encouraged by the hesitation and slowness of his rival, who lost precious weeks in Greece, Octavius decided to attack as soon as possible. Thus, his fleet left the port of Brindisi (southeast of Italy) and crossed the Ionian Sea towards the headland. His objective was to speed to Actium where the fleet of his opponent was stationed in order to seize it. At that time, part of the land army of Mark Antony had not yet arrived in Actium, which worried the Roman general. Yet, Octavius hesitated and did not attack, instead deciding to set up a blockade around the harbor to enclose the fleet of Mark Antony in the harbor of Actium.

THE FORCES PRESENT

Mark Antony possessed 300 very large ships, along with 200 Egyptian ships, which were smaller and more manageable. According to Plutarch (Greek writer, 50-125 A.D.), his army consisted of nearly 200 000 men, which gave him a considerable advantage on land. Mark Antony could also count on a few slingers (stone throwers), velites (spear throwers) and many archers on foot.

The 400 Roman ships were smaller, making them very fast and easy to maneuver. Octavius had a force of 80 000 soldiers: he therefore possessed greater means. However, the fleet of Octavius was conducted by professional sailors, while his opponent's was composed of infantry and cavalry members enlisted in the emergency. Therefore, the difference would be made by the naval combat.

A LAND OR NAVAL BATTLE?

While Mark Antony possessed superior powers to those of Octavius on land, he decided to fight at sea. Modern historians have long wondered about the reasons for this decision, which was fraught with consequences as it led to his downfall. Octavius' propaganda simply used irony and underlined the weakness of this opponent who wished to satisfy Cleopatra. Moreover, his lieutenants apparently urged him to fight on land, as their ships were too large to be properly operated, lacking rowers and sailors. He was also obliged to hire inexperienced men in Greece to make up the crews. In addition, the Roman legionnaires that followed him were very unaccustomed to naval battles. Nonetheless, it was Cleopatra's opinion that finally prevailed. For her, the battle should take place at sea. Indeed, she wanted to leave Actium as soon as possible in order to regain Egypt, which she had left leaderless for too long. Mark Antony was also facing new problems: desertion and malaria were rampant in his army, which further limited the number of sailors capable of fighting.

As for Octavius, he intended to deliver a decisive battle at Actium, while, for his opponents, the fighting was supposed to be nothing more than a skirmish, to allow them to flee from Actium in order to better reunite and fight on land. Therefore, Mark Antony was counting on a quick battle with minimal soldier losses, as he was convinced that the technical superiority of his vessels would give him a decisive advantage.

THE CLASH

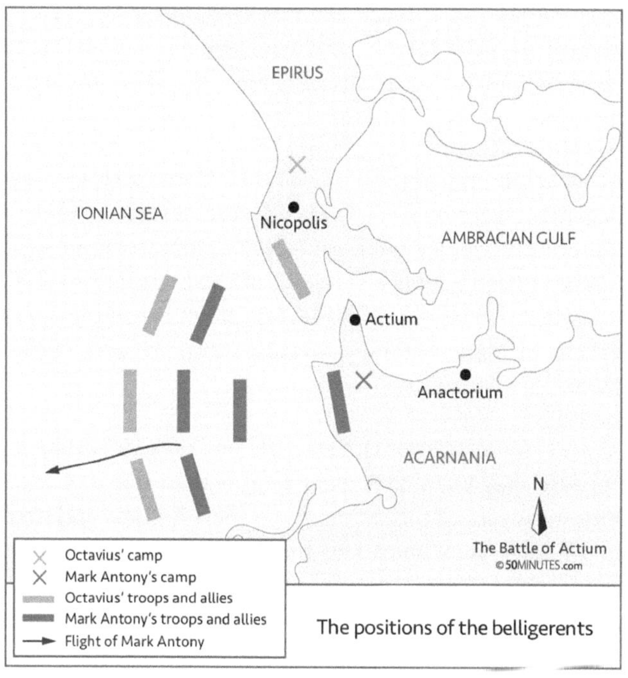

When the hostilities began, Octavius, Cleopatra and Mark Antony were all present on the battlefield. It seems that Mark Antony had high towers built on his ships so that his crew – among which were a multitude of archers and slingers – could fight as if on top of a wall.

Octavius and his faithful friend Marcus Vipsanius Agrippa carefully watched the enemy fleet. They ordered their vessels to stay clear of their opponents, around 1.5km away, so that the projectiles would not reach them. If he wanted to force his way through the blockade, Mark Antony was obliged to move forward and had only one possibility: to leave Actium and rush out to the open sea where his opponent was.

After some intimidation maneuvers, Mark Antony's fleet began to move and sped towards the vessels of Marcus Vipsanius Agrippa. Agrippa ordered his ships to retreat even further to attract the enemy out of the harbor of Actium, towards the deep sea. The goal was simple: lead the heavy galleys of Mark Antony seaward to disperse and scatter them.

At first, the vessels of Octavius did not seek direct impact because they knew they were weaker than those of Mark Antony. Aware of this, Marcus Vipsanius Agrippa preferred to gather several ships and then pounce on the isolated enemy ships. Thus, Octavius' ships began by colliding with an enemy ship to create maximum damage, before interrupting their attack and quickly resuming the assault once joined by several other ships. Antony's ships were harassed on all sides: the battle was taking a clear direction, even before the boarding was ordered. With this tactic, Marcus Vipsanius Agrippa and Octavius demonstrated that the outcome of a battle did not only depend on numerical and technical superiority.

The heavy vessels of Mark Antony defended themselves like besieged cities: they bombarded the enemy with a shower of stones, arrows and spears from their towers. Their striking power allowed them to quickly sink the ships of Octavius, but their accuracy and the speed of their action was too weak to prove truly effective.

CLEOPATRA'S RETREAT

The Battle of Actium.

The outcome of the conflict was still uncertain, as the tactic implemented by Marcus Vipsanius Agrippa required a lot of time. According to ancient historians, it was the flight of Cleopatra that precipitated the fate of the battle. Indeed, from the beginning of the attack, the queen was on her ship, behind the troops of Marc Antony. But although her ship was safe, she decided to hurriedly leave the battlefield. The queen of Egypt did not leave alone: she recalled her subjects by a signal so that they followed suit. The breakaway was so abrupt that the Egyptian vessels wreaked havoc in the ranks of Mark Antony's army. Even today, the turnaround is unexplained and an incomprehensible event. Latin sources, quick to condemn Cleopatra, argue that she fled because, due to the slowness of the fighting, she would have succumbed to feminine impatience.

THE FLIGHT OF MARK ANTONY

Noticing the flight of his beloved, Mark Antony also decided to leave the battlefield. He abandoned his own troops in the middle of the fighting, after climbing into a small galley to quickly join Cleopatra's ship. Although the general was safe and sound, he had just lost his honor.

Despite this departure, the battle raged on. Marcus Vipsanius Agrippa continued his tactics of attack, but Mark Antony's fleet was resistant. In order to speed up events, Octavius ordered the storming of the enemy ships. The boarding could therefore take place and the hand-to-hand combat could begin. In the confusion, all weapons were used: axes, swords, stones, etc. However, the soldiers of Mark Antony managed to repel the attackers. To regain the advantage, Octavius' men then launched flaming arrows and tried to burn down the enemy ships with pitch (highly flammable substance). It was ultimately this tactic that overwhelmed the forces of Mark Antony. Aided by the wind that had just picked up, the fire spread through many ships. Many of Mark Antony's soldiers died suffocating from the smoke of the fire. Since the fight no longer had a purpose, Mark Antony's soldiers agreed to lay down their arms and surrender. Octavius had just won the most important battle of his life.

The historian Plutarch believed that Mark Antony's army lost around 5 000 men and 300 vessels, while Paul Orosius (Spanish priest, 390-418) suggested that there were 13 000 dead. Within the army of Octavius, the figures remain unknown: no ancient author mentioned how many men perished on the winning side. However, historians assume that the losses were significant as the conflict was long undecided.

After a long battle, Octavius could now savor his victory: the Roman world was now at his feet.

REPERCUSSIONS OF THE BATTLE

THE DISAPPEARANCE OF OCTAVIUS' RIVALS

Mark Antony and Cleopatra fled Actium and sailed to Egypt. Some of Octavius' ships did try to engage in their pursuit to capture them, but did not succeed. Back in Alexandria, Mark Antony sank into a deep depression following his behavior during the battle. Cleopatra, meanwhile, tried to save what was left, but the situation was desperate: her allies gradually turned their backs on her and surrendered to Octavius in order to avoid his revenge.

A year after the battle, while Octavius directed his troops to Egypt, Mark Antony and Cleopatra sought in vain to negotiate with him. Octavius then declared himself ready to negotiate with the Egyptian queen if she consented to have her lover executed or banished him from Egypt. The thing that mattered most in Cleopatra's eyes was that her son Caesarion was not killed and that her children could have access to the throne of Egypt after her death. Therefore, she spread the false news of her suicide to Mark Antony, so that he would also opt for this end.

Abandoned by all his followers and his beloved, Mark Antony decided to end his days, plunging a sword into his chest. Seriously wounded, he was carried to Cleopatra, still alive, and died on 1 August 30 B.C. In Rome, it was said of him that he redeemed his cowardice with this heroic death.

Hearing of the death of his rival, Octavius wanted Cleopatra to be brought to Roma alive at any cost, so that he could parade her as a captive in his triumph. He then met with her and promised that she would be treated well if she agreed not to end her life, which she pretended to accept. A few days later, she committed suicide.

OCTAVIUS, SOLE RULER OF ROME AND FUTURE EMPEROR

Octavius wanted to present himself as the unifier of the Romans and the peacemaker of the world. Soon after the Battle of Actium, he incorporated the surviving Roman soldiers of Mark Antony's army into his own. Wanting to punish the provinces, cities and kingdoms that had supported his rival, Octavius imposed heavy taxes. Upon learning of the death of Cleopatra, he reduced Egypt to a Roman province, thus marking the end of the Ptolemaic dynasty (family of Cleopatra), which had ruled the country for 270 years.

Although Octavius proved generous to the three children that Mark Antony had with Cleopatra, he was intractable with Caesarion. Indeed, the child was executed shortly after the death of his mother, as Octavius judged that it would have been dangerous to let the alleged son of Julius Caesar live.

The consequences of the battle were also politically significant: Octavius was now unrivaled and his victory ensured him control of the Mediterranean. The Battle of Actium put an end to the period of civil wars that had struck Rome long ago. The time of the struggles between the Romans for supreme power was now gone.

The Battle of Actium signaled the death of the aristocratic Republic which had governed Rome for many years. However, it was after a century of political developments that Octavius established the principate in 27 B.C. The battle only accelerated the process of the concentration of power by eliminating his last rival. Some historians point out that, from the time of Julius Caesar, the political regime had been replaced by a monarchy. Does this mean that Octavius imagined, when he took the name of Augustus, that the imperial model would survive for centuries and dominate the West and the East for a long time? There is cause to doubt this.

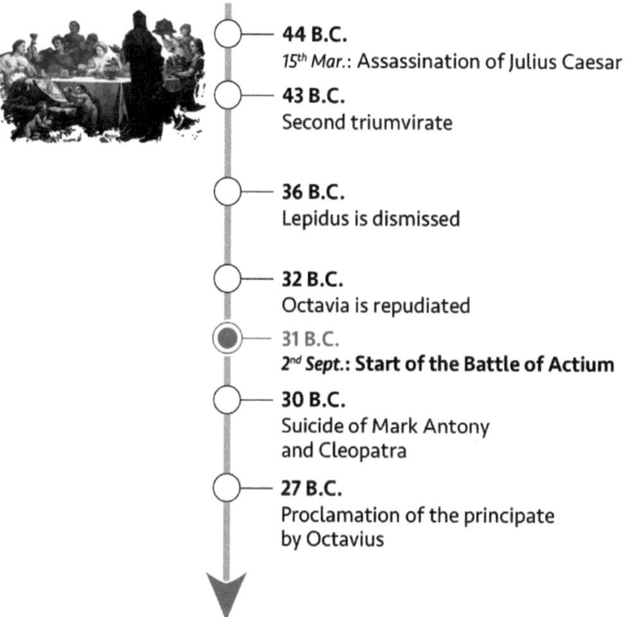

44 B.C.
15th Mar.: Assassination of Julius Caesar

43 B.C.
Second triumvirate

36 B.C.
Lepidus is dismissed

32 B.C.
Octavia is repudiated

31 B.C.
2nd Sept.: **Start of the Battle of Actium**

30 B.C.
Suicide of Mark Antony
and Cleopatra

27 B.C.
Proclamation of the principate
by Octavius

- On 15 March 44 B.C., Julius Caesar was stabbed in public. The assassination was led by Gaius Cassius Longinus and Marcus Junius Brutus, the adopted heir of Julius Caesar.
- Thus began a struggle aimed at combating the two murderers. To do this, a new triumvirate was formed that bound Mark Antony, Octavius and Lepidus. Caesar's murderers were finally defeated in the Battle of Philippi in 42 B.C.
- Two years later, Octavius accused Lepidus of abusing his

powers, deposed him and confiscated his possessions for himself, which did not please Mark Antony.

- While Antony prepared to wage a war against the Parthians, he summoned Cleopatra to Cilicia. The latter was accused of having helped Marcus Junius Brutus and Gaius Cassius Longinus after the assassination of Julius Caesar. Aware of the diplomatic issue, she decided to use her charms to win the favor of the Roman politician.
- Becoming a true Hellenistic monarch, Antony made unbearable decisions for the Romans. Despite his marriage to Octavia, he conducted a romantic relationship with Cleopatra and offered some Roman territory to the children he bore with his lover.
- The situation was hardly improved when in 32 B.C., Mark Antony repudiated his wife. This was too much for Octavius, who managed to rally the Senate to begin a war against Cleopatra through the reading of Mark Antony's will.
- In both camps, preparations were well underway. A few days before the attack, Mark Antony had 500 vessels, most of which were difficult to manage due to their size, and about 200 000 men. As for Octavius, he possessed 400 smaller and faster vessels, and led around 80 000 men.
- Although Mark Antony was more prepared to fight on land, he agreed with the opinion of Cleopatra who wanted it to be a naval battle.
- The conflict began on 2 September 31 B.C. The tactics implemented by Marcus Vipsanius Agrippa was to constantly harass the vessels of Mark Antony, and although they managed to defend themselves, this showed

little effect.

- The fate of the battle was precipitated by the flight of Cleopatra, who was soon joined by Mark Antony. Octavius' side took advantage of this unexpected turn of events to gain the upper hand. With their flaming arrows, they managed to burn the enemy ships. The battle was thus won.
- A year later, while Octavius' troops entered Alexandria to stop Mark Antony and Cleopatra, they both committed suicide. Octavius became the sole ruler of Rome. In 27 B.C. he established the principate and took the name Augustus.

We want to hear from you!
Leave a comment on your online library
and share your favourite books on social media!

FIND OUT MORE

BIBLIOGRAPHY

* Cassius Dio (2014) *Complete Works of Cassius Dio*. Delphi Classics.
* Juvenal (2008) *The Satires*. Trans. Rudd, N. Oxford: Oxford World's Classics.
* Marcus Velleius Paterculus (1982) *Histoire romaine*. Paris: Les Belles Lettres.
* Plutarch (2015) *Lives of the Noble Grecians and Romans*. Trans. Clough, A.H. Oxford: Benediction Classics.
* Suetonius (2007) *The Twelve Caesars*. Trans. Graves, R. and Rives, J.B. London: Penguin.
* Tacitus (2003) *The Annals of Imperial Rome*. Trans. Grant, M. London: Penguin.
* Tacitus (2008) *The Histories*. Trans. Fyfe, W.H. Oxford: Oxford World's Classics.
* Virgil (2003), *The Aeneid*. Trans. West, D. London: Penguin.

ADDITIONAL SOURCES

* Chaveau, M. (2000) *Egypt in the Age of Cleopatra: History and Society Under Ptolemies*. Trans. Lorton, D. New York: Cornell University Press.
* Chaveau, M. (2002) *Cleopatra: Beyond the Myth*. Trans. Lorton, D. New York: Cornell University Press.
* Fratantuono, L. (2016) *The Battle of Actium 31 B.C.: War for the World*. Barnsley: Pen and Sword.
* Green, P. (1994) *Alexander to Actium: The Hellenistic Age*.

London: Thames & Hudson.
- Weigall, A. (2015) *The Life and Times of Marc Antony*. New York: Palatine Press.

ICONOGRAPHIC SOURCES

- *The Death of Caesar*, painting by Jean-Léon Gérôme, 1867. Royalty-free reproduction picture.
- *The Meal of Marc Antony and Cleopatra, painting by* Charles-Joseph Natoire, 1754. Royalty-free reproduction picture.
- The Battle of Actium. © Erica Guilane-Nachez – Fotolia.com.

PLAYS

- Shakespeare, W. (2008) *Anthony and Cleopatra*. Oxford: Oxford World's Classics.

FILMS

- *Cleopatra*. (1934) [Film]. Cecil B. DeMille. Dir. USA: Paramount Pictures.
- *Cleopatra*. (1963) [Film]. Joseph L. Mankiewicz. Dir. USA: Twentieth Century Fox, MCL Films S.A., Walwa Films S.A.
- *Rome*. (2005-2007) [Television series]. John Milius, William J. Mac Donald and Bruno Hello. USA/Great Britain/Italy: HBO/BBC/Rai Fiction.

COMMEMORATIVE BUILDINGS

- The ruins of Nicopolis, city founded by Octavius in order to commemorate his victory at the Battle of Actium, at the entrance of the Ambracian Gulf (Greece).